GW01374519

Published by Emain Publications Limited, 2014.

Author & Illustrator Aidan Gormley.

Copyright © Aidan Gormley, 2014.

Original illustrations © Aidan Gormley

All Rights Reserved.

Design and Illustrations by Gary Boyd.

A CIP catalogue record for this book is available
from the British Library.

ISBN: 978-0-9573926-5-6

All rights reserved. This publication may
not be reproduced, stored in a retrieval system,
or transmitted in any form or by any means, electronic, mechanical,
photocopying, recording
or otherwise, without the prior written permission
of Emain Publications.

Printed by Minprint
in Northern Ireland

EMAIN
PUBLICATIONS

FERRARI ADVENTURE

BY
AIDAN GORMLEY

Once upon a time there was a little boy called Johnny and his favourite hobby was playing with fast cars. He was playing in the garden with his favourite car, which was a ... **red Ferrari**

He was dreaming about owning his own
Ferrari garage when he was all grown up
and had a good job
with lots and lots of money.

Suddenly there was a very loud **bang** and a flash of lightning and there in front of Johnny's eyes was a lifesize beautiful Formula 1 red Ferrari!!!

Johnny couldn't believe it! He looked at it...

He looked at it stunned in amazement!

Johnny ran over and jumped into the driver's seat.

Before he had time to look around him at the inside of this amazing car,
the engine revved giving out the most magnificent **roooar!** and off he sped!

He **whizzed** past houses and shops, schools and parks.
He whizzed up streets and down streets, up hills and down hills,
over bridges and under flyovers like lightning!

Everyone turned to look!!!

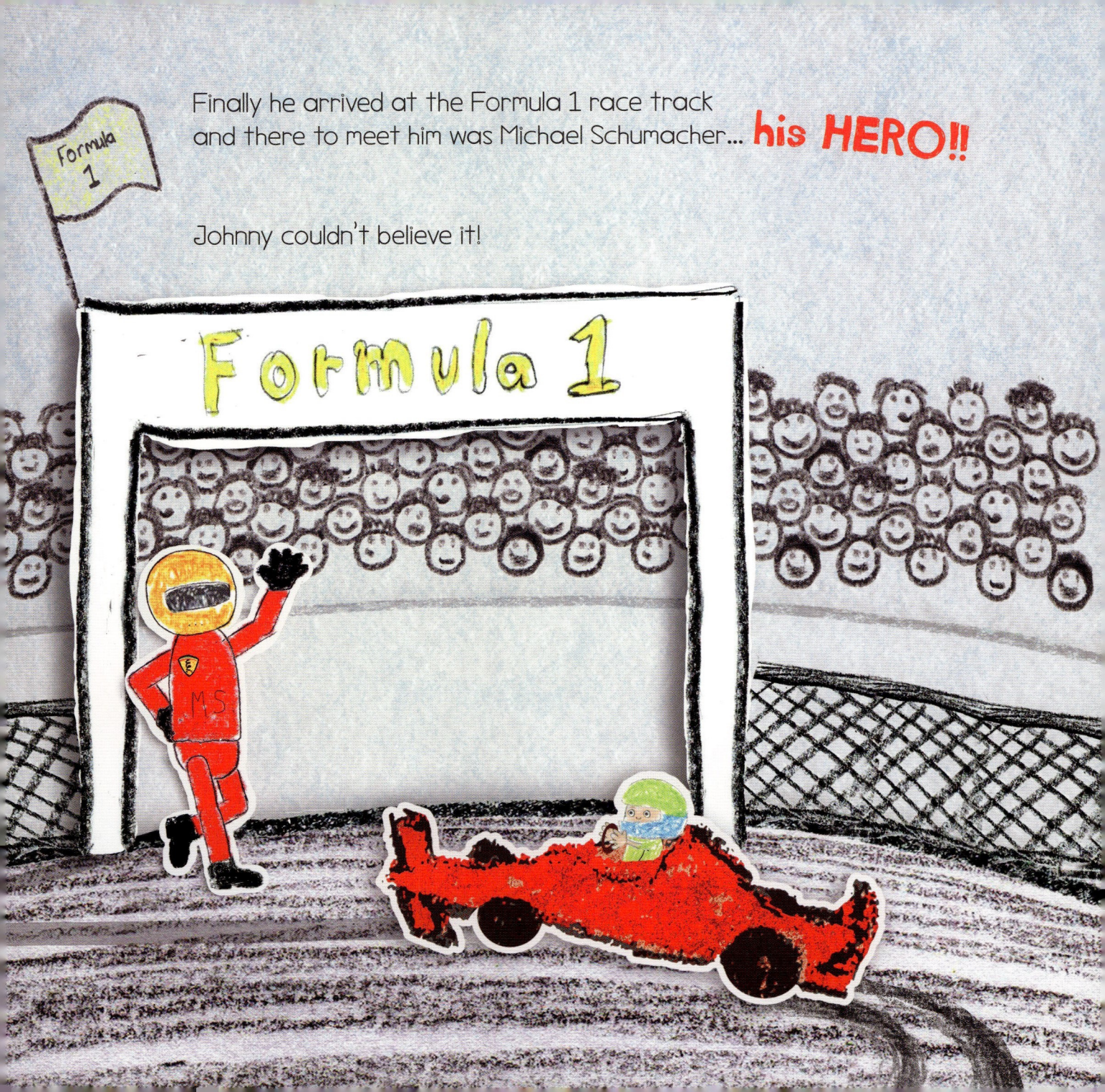

Finally he arrived at the Formula 1 race track and there to meet him was Michael Schumacher... his HERO!!

Johnny couldn't believe it!

The lights turned from **red** to **green** and the horn sounded and the race began.

Johnny was racing against his hero and lots of other famous Formula 1 drivers.

The race started off badly and Johnny was last.
This can't be happening! he thought.
He put his shoe down fully on the throttle and built up his speed,
whizzing past this driver and that driver!
Where was Michael Schumacher?
He had to beat him!

Circuit after circuit he gave it everything he had!!

It was the final circuit and he was catching up! Could he do it?

He was breathing heavily and his heart was racing!

He was **shaking** with excitment!

He was now driving beside his hero and was just about to pass him, when he heard a loud **knock**

and his name being called out!

Johnny!

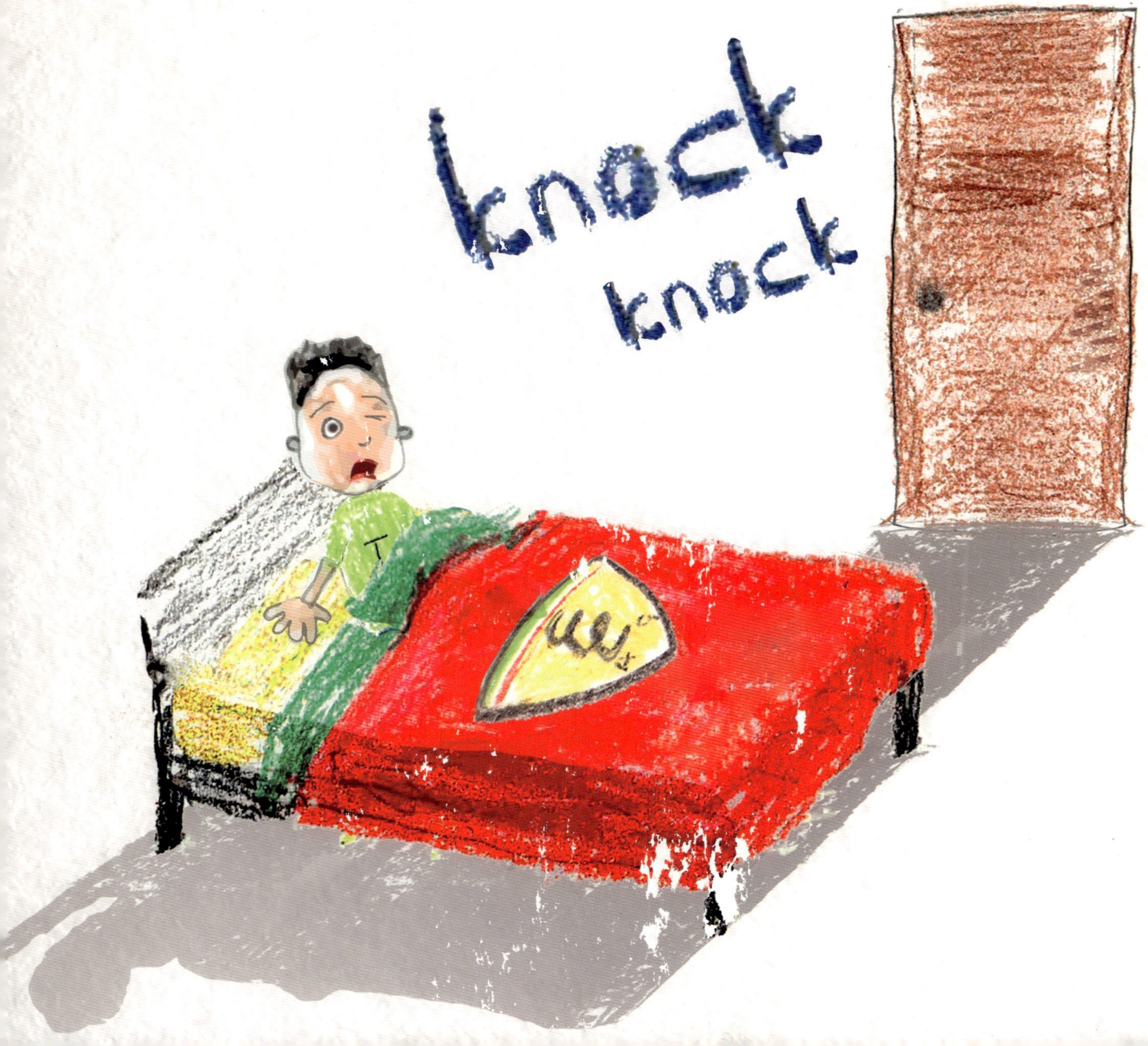
knock
knock